EXPLORE
my world

Penguins

Jill Esbaum

NATIONAL
GEOGRAPHIC
KiDS

WASHINGTON, D.C.

An emperor penguin!

For these penguins, Antarctica is home sweet home.

It's a frozen, snowy place without lakes or rivers or a single blade of anything green.

Waddle!

This tall-as-a-first-grader bird doesn't mind that the temperatures are below zero—*waaaay* below zero.

Their bodies are perfect for a refrigerated life.

A baby penguin would not survive long in this frozen world by itself. Luckily, emperor parents know how to protect their little one.

After Mom lays an egg, she rolls it from her webbed feet onto Dad's. Oops, careful!

When the egg is safely atop Dad's feet—whew!—he lowers a special feathered pouch to keep it cozy.

9

Mom leaves right away.
She needs to find food,
and for that, she must
travel to the sea.

She will walk many miles before reaching water. Her leathery feet march across the snow. Her sharp claws grip icy spots.

When she finds the sea, Mom will feast for weeks.

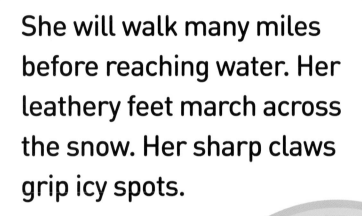

Brrr. Why Antarctica?

Can you waddle like a penguin?

How can penguins live in Antarctica?

Leathery, webbed feet are great for standing on ice and swimming!

How do you keep your feet warm?

Feathers are tightly packed and waterproof. Underneath, a layer of fat called blubber helps protect against the *ch-ch-chill.*

Is your hair waterproof?

Are your legs shorter or longer than a penguin's?

Shiver!

Bone-chilling cold.
Icy winds. Blizzards.

14

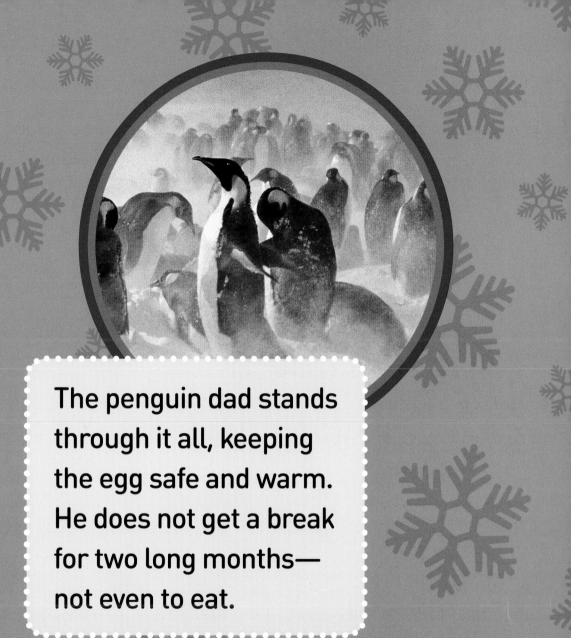

The penguin dad stands through it all, keeping the egg safe and warm. He does not get a break for two long months— not even to eat.

To keep from freezing, all the father penguins in a group, or colony, huddle close together. They take turns shuffling into the toasty middle, then out again.

Mom penguin returns to the colony in July or August. She and Dad call back and forth until they find each other.

Why, hello, chick!

As soon as Mom tucks the hatchling into her own feathered pouch . . . Dad takes off. It's his turn to find the sea and much needed food.

Like Mom, he waddle-walks over miles of ice and snow. He sometimes flops forward to toboggan, pushing with his feet and flippers.

What's for Lunch?

Would penguins eat carrots?

Do you eat fish?

What do emperor penguins eat?

Penguins eat food found only in the sea, like Antarctic silverfish, hooked squid, and Antarctic krill.

From their colony, penguins might have to walk 50 miles (80 km) to find open (unfrozen) water.

They dive deeper than any other bird—to 1,850 feet (565 m). And they're able to stay underwater for 15 to 20 minutes without taking a breath!

Can you swim underwater?

Should you walk on ice quickly or slowly?

Glurp!

Mom penguin's belly is still full of seafood. She brings bits up into her mouth to feed her chick.

The fuzzy chick grows bigger. Braver. It pops out to take a look at the wide, white neighborhood and toddles over the snow to meet new friends!

Summer arrives in December, and ice near the colony breaks up. An adult penguin chicksits while Mom goes off to fish.

Dive, penguin!

At last the penguin is big enough to try swimming and fishing on its own. *Sploosh!*

Penguin Map

There are 17 different types of penguins! Most of them live in Earth's Southern Hemisphere along the coast. Follow the key below to see where on Earth some of these penguins live.

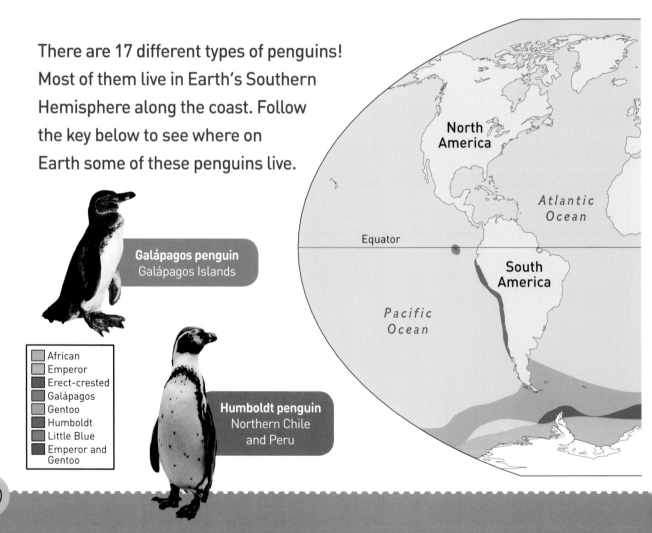

Galápagos penguin
Galápagos Islands

Humboldt penguin
Northern Chile and Peru

- ▢ African
- ▢ Emperor
- ▢ Erect-crested
- ▢ Galápagos
- ▢ Gentoo
- ▢ Humboldt
- ▢ Little Blue
- ▢ Emperor and Gentoo

North America

Atlantic Ocean

Equator

South America

Pacific Ocean

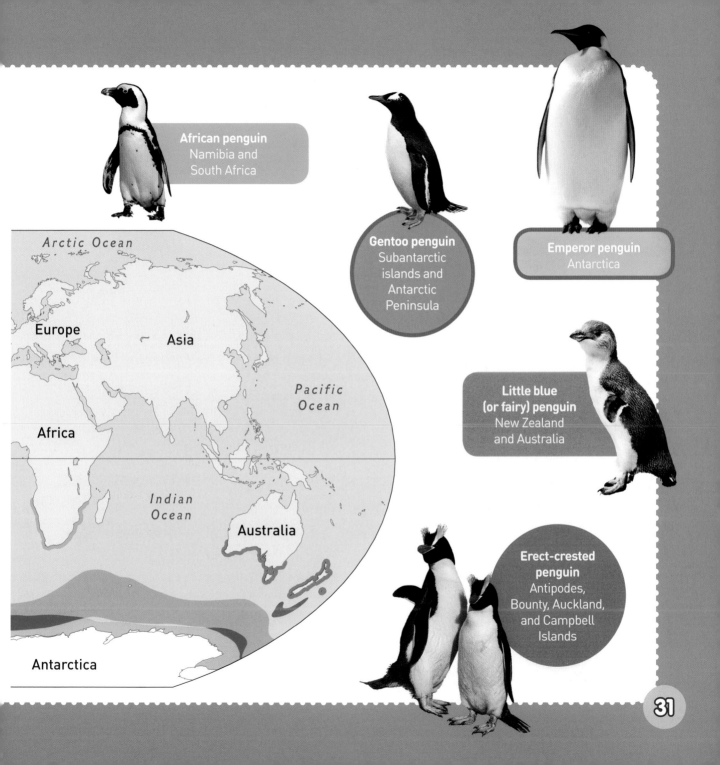

African penguin
Namibia and
South Africa

Gentoo penguin
Subantarctic
islands and
Antarctic
Peninsula

Emperor penguin
Antarctica

**Little blue
(or fairy) penguin**
New Zealand
and Australia

**Erect-crested
penguin**
Antipodes,
Bounty, Auckland,
and Campbell
Islands

Arctic Ocean

Europe

Asia

Pacific
Ocean

Africa

Indian
Ocean

Australia

Antarctica

For Grant and Olivia
—JE

Editor: Ariane Szu-Tu
Art Director: Amanda Larsen
Photography Editor: Lori Epstein

National Geographic supports K-12 educators with ELA Common Core Resources. Visit www.natgeoed.org/commoncore for more information.

Trade paperback ISBN: 978-1-4263-1701-9

Reinforced library binding ISBN: 978-1-4263-1702-6

The publisher gratefully acknowledges Dr. Gerald Kooyman of Scripps Institution of Oceanography and early education expert Catherine Hughes for their expert review of the book.

ILLUSTRATIONS CREDITS

Cover, Frans Lanting/Mint Images/Getty Images; back cover, J.-L. Klein & M.-L. Hubert/Biosphoto/Minden Pictures; 1, David Tipling/naturepl.com; 2–3, Tui De Roy/Minden Pictures; 4–5, W.Lynch/Arcticphoto.com; 6, Cordier Sylvain/hemis.fr/Getty Images; 7 (background), ivivankeulen/Shutterstock; 8, Fred Olivier/naturepl.com; 8 (background), Denis Barbulat/Shutterstock; 9, Pete Oxford/naturepl.com; 10, Paul Nicklen/National Geographic Creative; 11, Bob Smith/National Geographic Creative; 11 (background), ntnt/Shutterstock; 12 (UP), Paul Nicklen/National Geographic Creative; 12 (LO), Paul Nicklen/National Geographic Creative; 13 (LE), David Rootes/Arcticphoto.com; 13 (RT), blickwinkel/Alamy; 14, Frans Lanting/Mint Images/Getty Images; 15, Fritz Poelking/Picture Press RM/Getty Images; 16–17, Doug Allan/naturepl.com; 18 (UP), Jeff Wilson/naturepl.com; 18 (LO), Paul Souders/WorldFoto; 19, Doug Allen/naturepl.com; 20, Paul Souders/WorldFoto; 21, Armin Rose/Shutterstock; 22 (UP), Nattika/Shutterstock; 22 (CTR), pan-da3800/Shutterstock; 22 (LOLE), George F. Mobley/National Geographic Creative; 22 (LORT), Paul Nicklen/National Geographic Creative; 23 (UP), Frans Lanting/National Geographic Creative; 23 (LO), Paul Nicklen/National Geographic Creative; 24, Paul Nicklen/National Geographic Creative; 25 (UP), Paul Souders/WorldFoto; 25 (LO), J.-L. Klein & M.-L. Hubert/Biosphoto/Minden Pictures; 26, Sue Flood/naturepl.com; 27, Paul Nicklen/National Geographic Creative; 28–29, Paul Nicklen/National Geographic Creative; 30 (UP), gynane/iStockphoto; 30 (CTR), GoodOlga/iStockphoto; 30 (LO), Jeff Mauritzen/NGS; 31 (UP), Coldimages/iStockphoto; 31 (UP LE), George F. Mobley/National Geographic Creative; 31 (CTR), Stephen Meese/iStockphoto; 31 (LO), Tui De Roy/Minden Pictures; 32, Konrad Wothe/Minden Pictures

Printed in the United States of America
14/WOR/1